I0895853

POWER POSITIVITY

I AM CREATIVE

Quadrille

I BELIEVE WE ARE ALL BORN CREATIVE.

Henry Miller

CREATIVITY IS GETTING INSPIRATION AND HAVING THAT LIGHTNING BOLT IDEA MOMENT, AND THEN HAVING THE HARD WORK ETHIC TO SIT DOWN AT THE DESK AND WRITE IT DOWN.

Taylor Swift

THE ONLY THING YOU HAVE CONTROL OVER...

IS WHAT YOU CREATE.

Glen Powell

CREATIVE MINDS ARE RARELY TIDY.

John William Gardner

I'VE NEVER UNDERSTOOD THE TERM 'CREATIVE PERSON'. ALL PEOPLE ARE CREATIVE. THE DIFFICULTY IS THAT MOST OF US ARE UNAWARE OF OUR CREATIVE GIFTS.

Truman Capote

I BELIEVE TALENT IS LIKE ELECTRICITY. WE DON'T UNDERSTAND ELECTRICITY. WE USE IT.

Maya Angelou

ANY ACTIVITY BECOMES CREATIVE WHEN THE DOER CARES ABOUT DOING IT RIGHT, OR BETTER.

John Updike

CREATION IS EMBARRASSING. FOR EVERY NEW GOOD IDEA YOU HAVE, THERE ARE A HUNDRED, TEN THOUSAND FOOLISH ONES, WHICH YOU NATURALLY DO NOT CARE TO DISPLAY.

Isaac Asimov

IN ORDER TO CREATE A WORK OF ART, YOU NEED AN ARTIST, AN OBJECT, THE WORK, AND THE AUDIENCE. INDEED, WHERE THERE'S NO AUDIENCE, THERE'S NO ARTIST.

Henri Matisse

I JUST WRITE SO MANY BAD SONGS, AND I THINK THAT'S HOW YOU GET TO THE GOOD ONES...

I THINK SHOWING THE CREATIVE GODS THAT YOU'RE THERE, SHOWING UP, READY TO DO THE WORK, GOES A LONG WAY.

Olivia Rodrigo

**DON'T THINK.
THINKING IS THE ENEMY
OF CREATIVITY. YOU CANNOT
INTELLECTUALISE CREATIVITY.**

Ray Bradbury

AS LONG AS I'M STAYING CREATIVE, I'M HAPPY.

Zendaya

THE WORST ENEMY TO CREATIVITY IS SELF-DOUBT.

Sylvia Plath

WE ALL HAVE THAT SMALL VOICE THAT TELLS US WE'RE RUBBISH, AND WE NEED TO LEARN WHEN TO SILENCE IT.

Fyfe Dangerfield

THE MOST IMPORTANT THING ABOUT CREATIVITY IS THAT YOU HONOUR YOUR CREATIVITY AND YOU DON'T EVER IGNORE IT.

Lady Gaga

I LOVE TO LAUGH, I LOVE COLOUR, I LOVE TEXTURE, AND I LOVE CREATIVITY, SO I WAS ALWAYS INSPIRED BY PEOPLE WHO INCORPORATE THOSE THINGS IN THEIR WORK.

RuPaul

I'VE BEEN LUCKY THAT I'VE BEEN ABLE TO SPEAK THROUGH MY ART, IN MY VOICE, AND NOT HOLD BACK. IN THE MUSIC WORLD, YOU DEPEND ON YOURSELF FOR ARTISTIC CREATIVITY AND FREEDOM.

Sabrina Carpenter

THERE'S NO BETTER INSPIRATION OR MOTIVATION FOR WORK THAN BEING IN LOVE. IT'S WHAT YOU DREAM OF AS A CREATIVE PERSON.

Neil Diamond

ALL OF US HAVE BOTH THE POTENTIAL, AND THE NEED, TO BE CREATIVE.

Dr Christian Rominger

IT'S LESS ABOUT PUTTING PRESSURE ON YOURSELF TO BE THIS CREATIVE GENIUS IN EVERY MOMENT, AND MORE SO ABOUT JUST CREATING.

Keke Palmer

IDEAS COME IN BITS AND PIECES.

Judith Kerr

IT'S AN AWESOME BUSINESS, TO CREATE AND SHARE AND DISPATCH AND PUT SOMETHING OUT THERE THAT'LL OUTLIVE US.

Matthew McConaughey

WE ARE ALL CREATIVE; IT IS JUST THAT SOME OF US CHOOSE NOT TO ALLOW OURSELVES OUT OF THE BOX.

Charlotte Church

CREATIVE WORK REQUIRES A LOYALTY AS COMPLETE AS THE LOYALTY OF WATER TO THE FORCE OF GRAVITY.

Mary Oliver

CREATIVITY IS OUR NORMAL AND FUNDAMENTAL WAY OF BEING.

Ben Okri

EVERYBODY WORKS IN A CREATIVE WAY IN ORDER TO SURVIVE LIFE.

Helen Cammock

CREATIVITY HAS GOT TO START WITH HUMANITY AND WHEN YOU'RE A HUMAN BEING, YOU FEEL, YOU SUFFER.

Marilyn Monroe

CREATIVITY IS GOING INTO THE UNCERTAIN, AND THE UNCERTAIN IS ALWAYS SCARY.

Elizabeth Gilbert

I HAVE A LOT OF PASSION. I HAVE A LOT OF SPIRITUAL ENERGY AND A LOT OF CREATIVE ENERGY. AND THAT'S A PRETTY BIG FORCE, ACTUALLY.

Dolly Parton

MANY PAINTERS ARE AFRAID OF THE BLANK CANVAS, BUT THE BLANK CANVAS IS AFRAID OF THE TRULY PASSIONATE PAINTER WHO DARES.

Vincent Van Gogh

SING IN THE SHOWER. DANCE TO THE RADIO. TELL STORIES. WRITE A POEM TO A FRIEND, EVEN A LOUSY POEM. DO IT AS WELL AS YOU POSSIBLY CAN. YOU WILL GET AN ENORMOUS REWARD. YOU WILL HAVE CREATED SOMETHING.

Kurt Vonnegut

I TAKE CREATIVITY VERY LITERALLY. IT IS IN EVERYTHING WE DO. I BELIEVE LAWYERS HAVE A CREATIVE FLOW. I BELIEVE THERE'S A CREATIVE FLOW IN MOTHERHOOD, OUR FAMILY DYNAMICS, OUR EMOTIONS, AND EVERYTHING.

Doechii

CREATIVITY IS A LIFE-BLOOD FOR PEOPLE.

Mike Leigh

IT'S SO IMPORTANT TO BE CREATIVE FOR YOUR OWN IDENTITY.

Kate Moss

BEING CREATIVE IS ABOUT HAVING FUN AND LOOKING AT LIFE THROUGH THE LENS OF A CHILD.

Taika Waititi

TO BE TRULY INSPIRED, YOU MUST LEARN TO TRUST YOUR INSTINCT, AND YOUR CREATIVE EMPATHY.

Tamara Rojo

FEELING INTIMIDATED IS A GOOD SIGN. WRITING FROM A PLACE OF SAFETY PRODUCES STUFF THAT IS, AT BEST, DULL AND, AT WORST, DISHONEST.

Lucy Prebble

OTHER CREATIVE PEOPLE ARE A RESOURCE THAT NEEDS TO BE EXPLOITED.

Anthony Neilson

IF YOU HAVE A GOOD IDEA, STICK TO IT.

Susan Philipsz

MISTAKES CAN BE INSPIRING – ALLOW YOURSELF TO TAKE RISKS AND DO WHAT SCARES YOU.

Kate Royal

DON'T THINK ABOUT IT, JUST DO IT – YOU REALLY DON'T NEED VERY MUCH TO BE CREATIVE.

Antony Gormley

CREATIVITY STARTS WITH TAKING A LEAP OF FAITH – TELLING YOUR FEARS THEY ARE NOT ALLOWED WHERE YOU ARE HEADED.

Beyoncé

LET YOURSELF SEE WHAT YOU'RE CAPABLE OF. WE HAVE TO, IF NOTHING ELSE, BE WILLING TO SEE WHAT WE CAN DO.

Taylor Jenkins Reid

THE MORE YOUR ART REFLECTS YOU, THE MORE IT WILL SPEAK TO OTHER PEOPLE. IF YOU ARE NOT SURE WHAT YOU SHOULD DO, JUST DO WHATEVER COMES INTO YOUR HEAD OR CATCHES YOUR IMAGINATION.

Michael Craig-Martin

THERE IS NOTHING AS EXCITING IN THIS WORLD AS ROAMING THE BEAUTIFUL WILDS OF THE HUMAN IMAGINATION.

Matt Haig

I'M LOOKING FOR CREATIVITY I HAVEN'T MATCHED YET, A FEELING I HAVEN'T FELT.

Kendrick Lamar

IN TIMES OF STRIFE, WE HAVE OUR IMAGINATION, WE HAVE OUR CREATIVE IMPULSE, WHICH ARE THINGS THAT ARE MORE IMPORTANT THAN MATERIAL THINGS. THEY ARE THE THINGS THAT WE SHOULD MAGNIFY.

Patti Smith

THE CRAFT IS SOMETHING YOU CAN WORK ON AND GROW, BUT IT'S JUST A TOOL. THE ACT OF WRITING, HAVING IDEAS OF VALUE AND MAKING ALBUMS, IS TRULY SOMETHING FROM THE HEART AND THE MIND THAT MOSTLY HAPPENS OUTSIDE THE STUDIO.

Jack Antonoff

AN IDEA IS JUST A MAP. THE ULTIMATE LANDSCAPE IS ONLY DISCOVERED WHEN IT'S UNDER FOOT.

Rupert Goold

THE NEED TO CREATE INTERESTING CREATIVE WORK, CREATIVE THINGS, CREATIVE HOBBIES MAKES ME EXCITED AND MAKES ADRENALINE PUMP THROUGH MY BODY.

Florence Pugh

IT IS VERY EXCITING TO JUST HAVE COMPLETE FREEDOM TO PURSUE WHATEVER MY CREATIVE APPETITE WANTS.

Chris Evans

CREATING AND COLLABORATING HAS BEEN PART OF MY SELF-DISCOVERY JOURNEY.

Millie Bobby Brown

I LOVE PAINTINGS TOO MUCH, LOVE COLOUR TOO MUCH, LOVE SEEING TOO MUCH, LOVE FEELING TOO MUCH, LOVE ART TOO MUCH, LOVE TOO MUCH.

Keith Haring

I DON'T HAVE TO WORK ON CREATIVITY, IT'S JUST THERE.

James Patterson

CREATION IS THE WELLSPRING OF LIFE.

Amiri Baraka

I FEEL MOST CREATIVELY FREE IN THE STUDIO. WRITING AND EXPERIMENTING WITH NEW SOUNDS ALWAYS GIVES ME A FEELING OF RELEASE.

Dua Lipa

I DON'T FOLLOW A ROUTINE OR A SCHEDULE, I THINK THAT HELPS MY CREATIVE PROCESS. THANKFULLY, THE PEOPLE IN MY LIFE FIND IT MORE ENDEARING THAN ANNOYING.

Colleen Hoover

CREATIVITY IS JUST CURIOSITY. IT'S TWO BUBBLES OF CURIOSITY BANGING INTO EACH OTHER AND CREATING SOMETHING NO ONE EVER CREATED BEFORE.

Richard Osman

BREAK THE MOULD! HAVE THE BIGGEST VISION YOU CAN!

IF YOU CAN'T DREAM IT, IT CANNOT OCCUR!

Judy Baca

FREEDOM IS NECESSARY FOR ME IN ORDER TO CREATE, AND IF I CANNOT CREATE I DON'T FEEL ALIVE.

Joni Mitchell

CREATIVITY IS A PROCESS, NOT AN EVENT.

James Clear

I WRITE BECAUSE IT FREES SOMETHING IN ME.

Kristin Hannah

DETERMINATION – NOT INSPIRATION – IS THE CHAUFFEUR OF CREATIVITY.

Margaret Atwood

I'M ALWAYS STRIVING TO FIGURE OUT WHERE I FIT IN THE WORLD AND HOW I CAN USE MY CREATIVITY AND MY VOICE TO CONNECT WITH PEOPLE.

Idina Menzel

CREATIVITY IS LOOKING AT A PROBLEM OR A SITUATION IN A DIFFERENT WAY FROM EVERYBODY ELSE, AND SEEING SOMETHING THEY HAVE MISSED.

Yuriko Yamamoto

IF YOU HAVE A VAGUE IDEA OF A SENTENCE, A SCENE, A PARAGRAPH, THE STORYLINE, JUST START WITH THAT. ANYTHING IS BETTER THAN NOTHING.

Marian Keyes

A HUNCH IS CREATIVITY TRYING TO TELL YOU SOMETHING.

Frank Capra

DON’T WAIT FOR PERMISSION TO DO SOMETHING CREATIVE.

Ava DuVernay

CREATIVITY IS ABUNDANT, BUT GREAT EXECUTION IS SCARCE.

Adam Grant

CREATE ART AND LIVE LIFE, WITH EQUAL COMMITMENT AND PASSION.

Renée Elise Goldsberry

COMMERCIAL AND CREATIVE SUCCESS ARE NOT THE SAME THING. THERE ARE ALL KINDS OF REASONS THAT A PERSON MIGHT FAIL IN THE MARKETPLACE THAT DON'T REALLY HAVE TO DO WITH THE QUALITY OF THEIR WORK.

Gabrielle Zevin

CREATIVITY IS VITAL FOR THE SOUL.

Ashley Roberts

CREATIVITY IS ALLOWING YOURSELF TO MAKE MISTAKES. ART IS KNOWING WHICH ONES TO KEEP.

Scott Adams

THE MOMENT THAT I WAS ABLE TO REALLY BE BRAVE IN THOSE MOMENTS...

AND STEP OUT AND CONQUER MY FEARS, I FOUND SUCH JOY IN BEING CREATIVE.

Phillipa Soo

A TRUE ARTIST IS NOT ONE WHO IS INSPIRED, BUT WHO WILL INSPIRE OTHERS.

Salvador Dalí

YOU ARE ONLY LIMITED BY YOUR IMAGINATION.

Malika Favre

ONLY PEOPLE WHO HAVE THE ARROGANCE OF CREATIVITY DARE TO REACH FOR THE HIGHEST POSSIBILITIES.

Abraham Maslow

CREATIVITY CAN BE DESCRIBED AS LETTING GO OF CERTAINTIES.

Gail Sheehy

YOU KNOW THE WONDERFUL THING ABOUT BEING CREATIVE? YOU GET TO USE YOUR VOICE AND EXPRESS YOURSELF.

Malorie Blackman

STICKING TO WHAT YOU KNOW IS A DISSERVICE TO YOUR OWN CREATIVITY.

Sarah Slutsky

YOU SHOULD BE CELEBRATED FOR YOUR CREATIVITY, FOR YOUR FEARLESSNESS, FOR YOUR PERSISTENCE AND DETERMINATION.

Rihanna

BEING CREATIVE IS THE MOST TREMENDOUS FUN. IT PASSES THE TIME, IF TIME HAS TO BE PASSED, IN AN ABSOLUTELY UNEQUALLED WAY.

Alexander McCall Smith

TO BE AN ARTIST YOU NEED COURAGE.

Yoko Ono

CREATIVITY CAN BE A WAY IN WHICH YOU DISCOVER MORE ABOUT YOURSELF. IT IS AN EXPRESSION OF YOURSELF, AND IT CAN BE THE LIFEBLOOD OF WHO YOU ARE.

Jude Law

INTUITION IS THE ESSENCE OF CREATIVITY.

Ingmar Bergman

THE IMPORTANCE OF ANY CREATIVE WORK IS TO EXPAND OUR VIEW OF THE WORLD WE ALL SHARE.

Michael Palin

EVERY CHILD IS AN ARTIST UNTIL...

HE'S TOLD HE'S NOT AN ARTIST.

John Lennon

CREATIVITY IS ONLY INTELLIGENCE HAVING FUN.

Joey Reiman

CREATIVITY IS CONTAGIOUS, PASS IT ON.

Albert Einstein

Quadrille, Penguin Random House UK,
One Embassy Gardens, 8 Viaduct
Gardens, London SW11 7BW

Quadrille Publishing Limited is part of the Penguin Random House group of companies whose addresses can be found at: global.penguinrandomhouse.com

Penguin Random House UK

Copyright © Quadrille 2025

Quadrille has asserted their right to be identified as the author of this Work in accordance with the Copyright, Designs and Patents Act 1988

No part of this book may be used or reproduced in any manner for the purpose of training artificial intelligence technologies or systems. In accordance with Article 4(3) of the DSM Directive 2019/790, Penguin Random House expressly reserves this work from the text and data mining exception.

Published by Quadrille in 2025

www.penguin.co.uk

A CIP catalogue record for this book is available from the British Library

ISBN 9781837833771

10 9 8 7 6 5 4 3 2 1

Managing Director, Publishing: Sarah Lavelle
Publishing Director: Kate Pollard
Senior Commissioning Editor: Kate Burkett
Assistant Editor: Harriet Thornley
Text curated by: Satu Fox
Designer: Claire Warner Studio
Production Manager: Sabeena Atchia

Colour reproduction by p2d

Printed in China by RR Donnelley Asia Printing Solution Limited

The authorised representative in the EEA is Penguin Random House Ireland, Morrison Chambers, 32 Nassau Street, Dublin D02 YH68.

FSC
www.fsc.org
MIX
Paper | Supporting responsible forestry
FSC® C018179

Penguin Random House is committed to a sustainable future for our business, our readers and our planet. This book is made from Forest Stewardship Council® certified paper.